Tax Diary
2018/2019

APRIL 2018

F	6	
S	7	
S	8	

		APRIL 2018
M	9	
T	10	
W	11	
T	12	
F	13	
S	14	
S	15	

APRIL 2018		
M	16	
T	17	
W	18	
T	19	
F	20	
S	21	
S	22	

APRIL 2018		
M	23	
T	24	
W	25	
T	26	
F	27	
S	28	
S	29	

APRIL/MAY 2018		
M	30	
T	1	
W	2	
T	3	
F	4	
S	5	
S	6	

MAY 2018

M	7	
T	8	
W	9	
T	10	
F	11	
S	12	
S	13	

MAY 2018

M	14	
T	15	
W	16	
T	17	
F	18	
S	19	
S	20	

MAY 2018		
M	21	
T	22	
W	23	
T	24	
F	25	
S	26	
S	27	

M	28	
T	29	
W	30	
T	31	
F	1	
S	2	
S	3	

MAY/JUNE 2018

JUNE 2018

M	4	
T	5	
W	6	
T	7	
F	8	
S	9	
S	10	

JUNE 2018

M	11	
T	12	
W	13	
T	14	
F	15	
S	16	
S	17	

JUNE 2018		
M	18	
T	19	
W	20	
T	21	
F	22	
S	23	
S	24	

JUNE/JULY 2018

M	25	
T	26	
W	27	
T	28	
F	29	
S	30	
S	1	

JULY 2018

M	2	
T	3	
W	4	
T	5	
F	6	
S	7	
S	8	

JULY 2018

M	9	
T	10	
W	11	
T	12	
F	13	
S	14	
S	15	

JULY 2018

M	16	
T	17	
W	18	
T	19	
F	20	
S	21	
S	22	

JULY 2018

M	23	
T	24	
W	25	
T	26	
F	27	
S	28	
S	29	

JULY/AUGUST 2018		
M	30	
T	31	
W	1	
T	2	
F	3	
S	4	
S	5	

AUGUST 2018		
M	6	
T	7	
W	8	
T	9	
F	10	
S	11	
S	12	

AUGUST 2018

M	13	
T	14	
W	15	
T	16	
F	17	
S	18	
S	19	

AUGUST 2018		
M	20	
T	21	
W	22	
T	23	
F	24	
S	25	
S	26	

AUGUST/SEPTEMBER 2018		
M	27	
T	28	
W	29	
T	30	
F	31	
S	1	
S	2	

SEPTEMBER 2018

M	3	
T	4	
W	5	
T	6	
F	7	
S	8	
S	9	

SEPTEMBER 2018

M	10	
T	11	
W	12	
T	13	
F	14	
S	15	
S	16	

SEPTEMBER 2018

M	17	
T	18	
W	19	
T	20	
F	21	
S	22	
S	23	

SEPTEMBER 2018		
M	24	
T	25	
W	26	
T	27	
F	28	
S	29	
S	30	

OCTOBER 2018

M	1	
T	2	
W	3	
T	4	
F	5	
S	6	
S	7	

OCTOBER 2018

M	8	
T	9	
W	10	
T	11	
F	12	
S	13	
S	14	

OCTOBER 2018

M	15	
T	16	
W	17	
T	18	
F	19	
S	20	
S	21	

OCTOBER 2018		
M	22	
T	23	
W	24	
T	25	
F	26	
S	27	
S	28	

OCTOBER/NOVEMBER 2018

M	29	
T	30	
W	31	
T	1	
F	2	
S	3	
S	4	

NOVEMBER 2018

M	5	
T	6	
W	7	
T	8	
F	9	
S	10	
S	11	

NOVEMBER 2018

M	12	
T	13	
W	14	
T	15	
F	16	
S	17	
S	18	

NOVEMBER 2018		
M	19	
T	20	
W	21	
T	22	
F	23	
S	24	
S	25	

NOVEMBER/DECEMBER 2018

M	26	
T	27	
W	28	
T	29	
F	30	
S	1	
S	2	

DECEMBER 2018

M	3	
T	4	
W	5	
T	6	
F	7	
S	8	
S	9	

DECEMBER 2018

M	10	
T	11	
W	12	
T	13	
F	14	
S	15	
S	16	

DECEMBER 2018

M	17	
T	18	
W	19	
T	20	
F	21	
S	22	
S	23	

DECEMBER 2018

M	24	
T	25	
W	26	
T	27	
F	28	
S	29	
S	30	

M	31	
T	1	
W	2	
T	3	
F	4	
S	5	
S	6	

DECEMBER 2018/JANUARY 2019

JANUARY 2019

M	7	
T	8	
W	9	
T	10	
F	11	
S	12	
S	13	

		JANUARY 2019
M	14	
T	15	
W	16	
T	17	
F	18	
S	19	
S	20	

JANUARY 2019

M	21	
T	22	
W	23	
T	24	
F	25	
S	26	
S	27	

	JANUARY/FEBRUARY 2019	
M	28	
T	29	
W	30	
T	31	
F	1	
S	2	
S	3	

FEBRUARY 2019

M	4	
T	5	
W	6	
T	7	
F	8	
S	9	
S	10	

FEBRUARY 2019

M	11	
T	12	
W	13	
T	14	
F	15	
S	16	
S	17	

FEBRUARY 2019

M	18	
T	19	
W	20	
T	21	
F	22	
S	23	
S	24	

FEBRUARY/MARCH 2019

M	25	
T	26	
W	27	
T	28	
F	1	
S	2	
S	3	

MARCH 2019

M	4	
T	5	
W	6	
T	7	
F	8	
S	9	
S	10	

MARCH 2019		
M	11	
T	12	
W	13	
T	14	
F	15	
S	16	
S	17	

MARCH 2019		
M	18	
T	19	
W	20	
T	21	
F	22	
S	23	
S	24	

MARCH 2019

M	25	
T	26	
W	27	
T	28	
F	29	
S	30	
S	31	

APRIL 2019

M	1	
T	2	
W	3	
T	4	
F	5	

www.ingramcontent.com/pod-product-compliance
Lightning Source LLC
Chambersburg PA
CBHW081227170526
45165CB00009B/2988